Trenace B. Lewis

Baby
Meets
Mary's
Little Lamb

AuthorHouse™
1663 Liberty Drive
Bloomington, IN 47403
www.authorhouse.com
Phone: 833-262-8899

Because of the dynamic nature of the Internet, any web addresses or links contained in this
book may have changed since publication and may no longer be valid. The views expressed
in this work are solely those of the author and do not necessarily reflect the views of the
publisher, and the publisher hereby disclaims any responsibility for them.

Any people depicted in stock imagery provided by Getty Images are models,
and such images are being used for illustrative purposes only.
Certain stock imagery © Getty Images.

Interior Image Credit: Sam Braden IV

Scripture taken from the New King James Version®. Copyright © 1982 by
Thomas Nelson. Used by permission. All rights reserved.

The Holy Bible, International Children's Bible® Copyright© 1986, 1988,
1999, 2015 by Tommy Nelson™, a division of Thomas Nelson.

This book is printed on acid-free paper.

ISBN: 978-1-6655-2207-6 (sc)
ISBN: 978-1-6655-3280-8 (hc)
ISBN: 978-1-6655-2208-3 (e)

Library of Congress Control Number: 2021907218

Print information available on the last page.

Published by AuthorHouse 07/21/2021

authorHOUSE®

Dedication

And the Lord said to Jehu, "Because you have done well in doing what is right in My sight … your sons shall sit on the throne of Israel **to the fourth generation**" (2 Kings 10:30 NKJV).

This book is dedicated to my parents, Ray P. and Pearl Y. Bazemore who did well in the sight of the Lord by giving us the foundation who is Jesus Christ and leaving behind a legacy of faith that we can build upon until Jesus returns.

Preface

Success in life will come more readily to the one who can answer these questions: Where did I come from? Why am I Here? Where am I going? When is the best time to begin discovering answers to these questions? From the womb, although it's never too late to do so. If you have yet to discover the answers to these questions for your own life you can do so while helping someone in the next, or future generations do the same. Remember, it takes a village to raise a child.

So, if you are a parent to be, a parent currently, or if you just desire to sow into the life of a child, be intentional in helping that blessed gift from God discover answers to life's most fundamental questions with a copy of "Baby Meets Mary's Little Lamb". This little book is the first in a series entitled, "The Black on Purpose Equity Series" designed to help you to help your "blessing" **unlock** the door to success! Each book can be personalized with a name and photograph to build memories and chart physical growth and development from generation to generation. Read it again and again and again as you unlock the door to your baby's potential and destiny. Turn the **key** today!

This book is presented to

On

Have a fantastic journey!!!

Place Photograph Here

Mary had a little lamb, little lamb, little lamb
Mary had a little lamb...

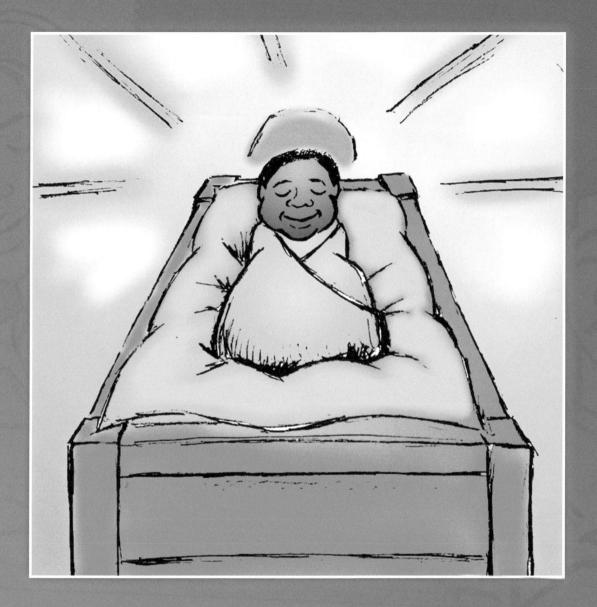

and JESUS was his name!!

For unto us a child is born; unto us a son is given...
Isaiah 9:6a NKJV

When He grew up, he went away, went away, went away...

Mary was sad, but Jesus knew he had not come to stay.

But I tell you the truth. It is better for you that I go
away. When I go away I will send the Helper to you. If I
do not go away, then the Helper will not come.

John 16:7 ICB

He sent to you a special gift, special gift, special gift
He sent to you a special gift....

... A Special, Special Friend!!!

Now you don't have to be afraid, be afraid, be afraid

He'll be with you wherever you go and help you every day!

I will ask the Father to give you a special friend who
will help you and be with you forever.
Cf. John 14:16

So, won't you come and follow him, follow him, follow him
He'll lead the way, close to him stay.
Your journey now begin!

These are the ones who follow the Lamb wherever He goes.
Revelation 14:4b NKJV

The Beginning...

Afterword

Yes! This is indeed the beginning of a great move of God. Today is Friday, January 8, 2021. As I reflect on the events of the past two days God is pouring out His Holy Spirit upon me afresh for this new day and I am filled with joy as my faith, hope, and trust in the sovereign God of the universe is renewed.

God, through the "changing of the guards" in the United States government is setting the stage for revival. This revival will come through the black church and through all who identify with the God of the black church no matter the color of their skin. Who is this God of the black church? He is the same God who in the beginning created the heavens and the earth. He is the same God who so loved the world that he gave us, Jesus Christ, his only begotten Son. He is the God of color, who sent us Jesus, a man of color to die for the sins of the world committed by human beings of EVERY color. He is the God of the red, yellow, black, brown, and white. All are equally precious in his sight!

Inequity has necessitated that the one true and living God be further distinguished as the God of the black church because black skin color has been stigmatized by traditional theological doctrine. The doctrine that black skin color is the result of a curse upon Ham, son of Noah, traditionally recognized as the progenitor of the black church is untrue and has contributed to the hatred and chaos that occurred on January 6, 2021.

The ancient Egyptians and Hebrews were a black people. The Israelites and Jews traditionally recognized as God's Chosen People have been dispersed to the four corners of the earth. The black church is a part of this dispersion. Yet, it is God's intent that, through evolution, miscegenation and conversion God's originally chosen people will no longer be identified by the flesh, meaning skin color, ethnicity, or culture, but by the spirit. Jew and Gentile will both be known by their fruit, simply because God has called us to love one another, to embrace and celebrate our differences, and to spend our time contributing our uniquely individual and uniquely cultural gifts to the body of Christ for the betterment of this world.

Racism in the church has been sustained by generational iniquity and by the traditional teaching and acceptance of a racist theology perpetuated by erroneous doctrine. As the first book in "The Black on Purpose Equity Series" this book "Baby Meets Mary's Little Lamb" is a baby step toward helping to correct this erroneous doctrine. It is my prayer that the end result will be a transformation from generational racial iniquity to generational racial reconciliation.

Jesus said, "If you continue in my word, then you are my disciples indeed and you shall know the truth and the truth will make you free" (cf. John 8:31-32). Please continue with us on our journey for truth as we navigate through "The Black on Purpose Equity Series".

The African American Pledge of Allegiance

When teaching our children to recite the Pledge of Allegiance, we must also teach them that "one nation, under God" means that we are black on purpose. To achieve one nation under God means understanding that God allowed our black ancestors to be imported from Africa to America, to be hated and to suffer physical and psychological indignities so that our powerfully united response of love, endurance, and resilience would be an emulation of the redemptive power of our Savior's love and that love will bring America, the New World in unity with Africa, the Old World even as the New Testament, through Christ came to fulfill the Old. The Pledge of Allegiance, and "Honor to Africa" when recited together shall be known as, "The African American's Pledge of Allegiance".

Honor to Africa

I give honor to Africa, home of the Garden of Eden, birthplace of humanity, and my ancestral home.

I shall forever respect Africa as the Motherland of God. For though the sorrow and the tears by which I came to be in this land are as deep as the ocean that brought me here, so also is the depth of God's purpose.

So, honor I not America, without remembering Africa. For my life has provided a bridge by which the old and the new shall forever be united in God, our Maker. So, I now...

Pledge allegiance to the flag of the United States of America

And to the Republic for which it stands... one nation under God,

Indivisible, with liberty and justice for all!

Printed in the United States
by Baker & Taylor Publisher Services